SUDDEN DEATH

ILLUSTRATED HISTORY OF WORLD CUP FOOTBALL AS A MYSTERY THRILLER
Part Three

Arun & Maha

CricketSoccer

This paperback edition first published in 2018
CricketSoccer
www.cricketsoccer.com

Copyright ©Arun and Maha

The right of Arun and Maha to be identified as the authors of this book has been asserted by them in accordance with the Copyright, Design and Patent Acts 1988

ISBN: 978-1732522626

Acknowledgements

The authors would like to express their sincerest thanks to the whole team associated with CricketSoccer, namely Tim Stannard, Faisal , Vieri Capretta, Paco Polit, Javed Ikbal, Avijit Sen and others, for their continuous support.

They would like to thank Meghana of Shadow Editing Services for her excellent work with the manuscript. Special gratitude to Uli Hesse and Kashinath Bhattacharjee for helping out with their immense knowledge. And finally, many thanks to Tanoy Dutta for his constant faith and encouragement.

Introduction

The history of the World Cup is full of riddles and mysteries. For instance, what happened to the original trophy, the Coupe Jules Rimet? If you scour the internet, you'll read that it was stolen from the headquarters of the Brazilian FA, melted into gold bars and sold. But this is probably nonsense. Pedro Berwanger, the policeman in charge of the investigation, pointed out that the cup as such was a lot more valuable than the gold it was made of. Which is why some people think that the trophy now sits on the shelf of a ruthless collector in some secret location.

Speaking of vanished objects, where is the ball from the 1954 final? The German FA claims it's in their shiny, large museum, but this is highly doubtful. The referee, William Ling, took possession of the ball after the game and for all we know, he still had it when he emigrated to Canada where he died in 1984. Most experts suspect the ball in the museum is from the semi-final or even just a ball used for training.
Men have vanished as well. Where is Joe Gaetjens, the man who scored one of the most famous World Cup goals of all time – the USA's 1-0 against England in 1950? In July 1964, he was arrested by the secret police in his native Haiti. That's the last we heard of him.

There are also numerous less sinister mysteries. What did Materazzi really say to Zidane in 2006? What did really happen to Ronaldo ahead of the 1998 final? Or what about the Mexican wave? We associate it with the 1986 World Cup, hence the name, but there is compelling evidence it was invented in 1981 and by a single man – an American called George Henderson. It should be called the Californian wave, really.
So it was about time that someone sat down to tell the story of the World Cup through riddles and mysteries. Or rather, through a mysterious man who speaks in riddles.

Arun (Arunabha Sengupta) has already proved he is up to the task with a novel in which none other than Sherlock Holmes solves a cricket case. But now, in this book by Arun and Maha, one man's brains are not enough – it takes an entire team of football experts and lovers to solve the riddles mentioned above and help save FIFA's money to ensure the next World Cup can be staged.

It means the book works on many levels. You can read it as a thriller or as a history book – or even as a puzzle book. Can you solve the riddles before FIFA's team can? Could I? Well, that must remain a mystery.

Uli Hesse

The Line up

Herr Fassler : Chief Financial Officer of FIFA, compulsive worrier

Mike Templeton: Football Historian, nibbler nonpareil

Sonja Bjarkardóttir: Genius code breaker, short-lipped and sassy

Javier Hernandez: Interpol Agent, cucumber-calm man of the world

FIFA is in turmoil. On the eve of the 2018 World Cup, the tournament is on the verge of falling through as a crazy football fan holds the organisation at ransom. It is up to these four curious characters to save the day.

With a few days to go for World Cup 2018, FIFA CFO Herr Fassler received a text message that kicked off a curious chain of events.

The systems of the organisation have been hacked into and the entire funds for the World Cup have been transferred to untraceable accounts.

Behind this diabolical manipulation is a football-tragic.

His demands:

A game of 20 questions

- The game will be played in 5 rounds
- Each round will have 4 questions based on the past World Cups
- At the end of each round, if you get all 4 questions correct, 20% of your funds will be transferred back to your account. You will be able to proceed to the next round.
- Any wrong answer ends the game. However, the funds already transferred, will remain with FIFA. The rest of the money will be lost.
- Questions will be asked every 2 hours
- Time permitted to answer each question is 15 minutes
- Timer will start automatically on your laptop

- The only way to recover your money and ensure the World Cup goes on exactly as planned is to answer all my questions correctly.

A crack team has been assembled
And they have recovered 40% of their funds by solving 8 questions

You can read all about that in

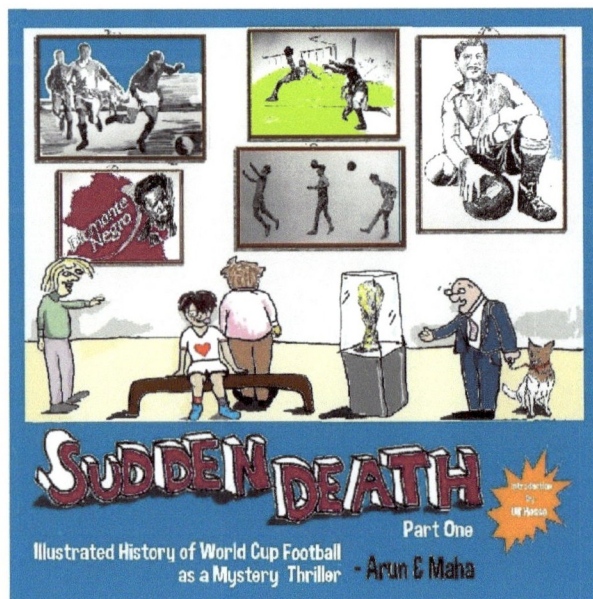

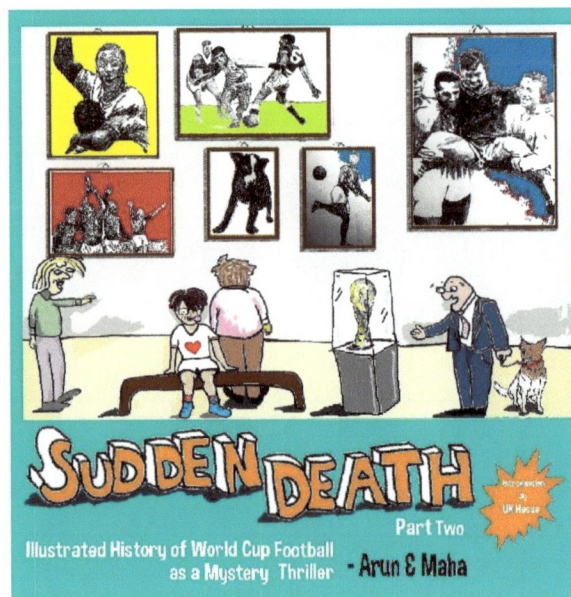

... and now

Strange to come into a graphic novel only to be part of self-referential drivel.

Did we just come face to face with our maker?

After life's highs there come the lows/Clasp hands behind and point with the nose

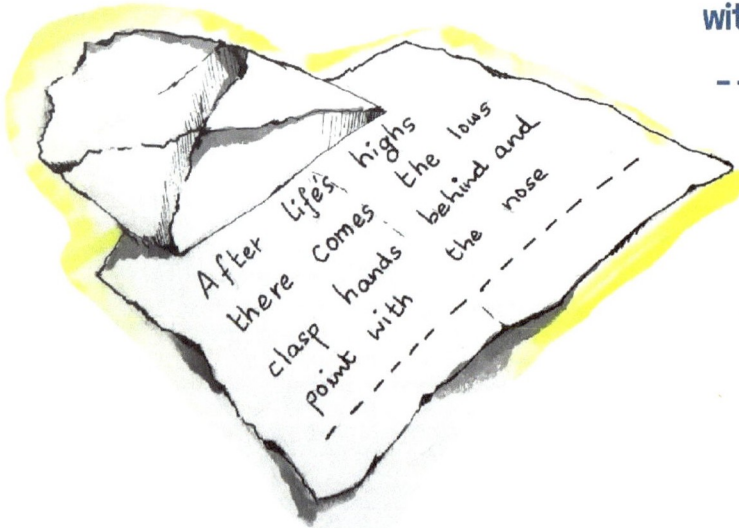

- - - - - - - - - - - - - -

Now, what happened in 1970?

After life's highs there comes the lows clasp hands behind and point with the nose
- - - - - -

1970, Mexico

Mexico. 200 peaceful demonstrators had been shot dead at Mexico City during the Olympics two years earlier. Plus there were problems with heat and altitude. It was an unusual choice as a venue.

But Mexico's status as hosts allowed another Central American country to take part. When El Salvador qualified, getting better of Honduras in three matches, there was a war between the nations. There were existing tensions between the neighbouring countries, but the immediate cause was football.

Yet, there was some great football, involved one of the greatest team ever seen and the fitting climax to the greatest football career of all time.

First Round

Group 1

Team	Mexico	Belgium	El Salvador	GF	GA	Pt
Russia	0-0(0-0)	4-1(1-0)	2-0(0-0)	6	1	5
Mexico		1-0 (1-0)	4-0(1-0)	5	0	5
Belgium			3-0(1-0)	4	5	2
El Salvador				0	9	0

Group 2

Team	Uruguay	Sweden	Israel	GF	GA	Pt
Italy	0-0(0-0)	1-0(1-0)	0-0(0-0)	1	0	4
Uruguay		0-1(0-0)	2-0(1-0)	2	1	3
Sweden			1-1(0-0)	2	2	3
Israel				1	3	2

Group 3

Team	England	Romania	Czechoslovakia	GF	GA	Pt
Brazil	1-0(0-0)	3-2(2-1)	4-1(1-1)	8	3	6
England		1-0(0-0)	1-0(0-0)	2	1	4
Romania			2-1(0-1)	4	5	2
Czechoslovakia				2	7	0

Group 4

Team	Peru	Bulgaria	Morocco	GF	GA	Pt
West Germany	3-1(3-1)	5-2(2-1)	2-1(0-1)	10	4	6
Peru		3-2 (0-1)	3-0(0-0)	7	5	4
Bulgaria			1-1(0-1)	5	9	1
Morocco				2	6	1

Highlights:

The Mexico-USSR match saw the use of the first ever substitute in a World Cup match. It was Russia's Anatoly Puzach, who replaced Vktor Serebrianikov after the first half.

El Salvador conceded their first goal to Mexico when the side stood still in protest to referee Ali Kandil's decision even while the hosts took the free kick. Juan Ignacio Basaguren became the first substitute to score a goal in a finals match.

Referee Airton Vieria de Moraes of Brazil was rumoured to have demanded money to favour Uruguay over Sweden. Although the investigations resulted in no proof, he was switched to the Israel-Italy match.

Joáo Saldanha, a journalist, had been so caustic about the national team that the administrators got pissed enough to make him the coach! He was replaced by Mário Zagallo when Saldanha was discovered at the house of another vehement critic, carrying a revolver.

Carlos Alberto, Jairzinho, Gérson, Pelé, Tostáo, Rivelino ... the Brazilian line-up was perhaps the greatest ever.

The save executed by Gordon Banks to tip a Pelé header over the bar was perhaps one of the greatest in World Cups. Only Banks observed: "I'm sure I've equalled that save in League games."

Several players, mainly from Bulgaria, Belgium and England, suffered severely from the conditions.

Quarter-Finals

Uruguay 1 (0,0) USSR 0 (0,0)
Italy 4 (1) Mexico 1 (1)
Brazil 4 (2) Peru 2 (1)
West Germany 3 (0,2) England 2 (1,2)

When Brazil faced Peru, the two coaches for the sides were Zagallo and Didi. The two of them had been teammates in Brazil's World Cup winning campaigns of 1958 and 1962.

Gordon Banks went down with food poisoning before the match against West Germany.

The British Prime Minister Harold Wilson blamed the result against West Germany as the reason for his loss in the General Election.

Semi-finals

Brazil 3 (1) Uruguay 1 (1)
After conceding a rather unnecessary goal in the 17th minute, Brazil's supreme frontline ran away with the match in the second half.

Italy 4 (1,1) West Germany 3 (0,1)
The heat and the altitude took its toll on the players as can be seen from the scoreline. In the 90th minute, West Germany equalised to take the match into extra-time. Very few of the players had the energy to continue through the next 30 minutes. In a see-saw battle, the Germans went up, Italy equalised and then took the lead again. Now Gerd Müller had scored his second goal in the match and the final of his prolific World Cup campaign to make it 3-3. However, a minute after that Rivera snatched the lead back for Italy. Beckenbauer played the last few minutes with his arm in sling as Italy held on to the lead.

Third Place Final

West Germany 1 (1) Uruguay 0(0)
Müller did not get the three required goals to touch Fontaine's record. However, he set up the goal that gave West Germany the third place.

Final

Brazil 4 (1) Italy 1 (1)
With the finalists having won the World Cup twice each, whoever won the final would keep the Jules Rimet Cup forever.

When Pelé scored the first goal from a header, it was Brazil's hundredth in the finals. But in spite of the brilliance of the forward line, one of the many lapses through the tournament saw Brazil relinquish the lead and the score was 1-1 at halftime.

In the second half Brazil conquered Italy and thereby the world. Pelé set up two more goals, the final one by Carlos Alberto, by the latter's confession, was possible only due to the near telepathic connection between the two. The Jules Rimet became Brazil's forever. Well, almost. In 1983, it was stolen and has not been recovered.

Highlights:

It is assumed that the Trophy, stolen in 1983, has been melted and sold.

Gérson, the Brazilian great, managed to play through the Cup despite smoking two packs of cigarette a day.

The final goal of the Cup, the one scored by Alberto, was known as the President's Goal, because General Emilio Garrasatazu Médici, president of Brazil, had predicted that they would score four.

Mário Zagallo became the first man to win the World Cup both as player and coach.

Top Scorer and Best Player 1970, Mexico

Der Bomber was a clinical finisher. One of the greatest goal-scorers of all time. In 2014 Miroslav Klose went past his German record of 68 goals, playing in his 132nd match. In contrast, Gerd Müller had netted those 68 in just 62 games.

With 10 goals in the 1970 World Cup, and four more in 1974, Müller also held the record for the highest number of goals in the history of the tournament before Ronaldo went past him in 2006.

He was noted for his incredible bursts of speed over short distances, although he came across as short, squat and unathletic and never seemed to run much. Hardly ever did he look the conventional footballer. But he was lethal in his acceleration and, in spite of his lack of inches, unbeatable in the air. Additionally, he had uncanny skills in turning quickly with perfect balance. All this was topped off by a supreme instinct of goal scoring.

He scored just once in the first match against Morocco, but quickly got into his groove with three against Bulgaria and a hat-trick against Peru. After an unimpressive showing through most of the quarter-final, his goal in the extra time pipped England. He scored two more, both in the extra-time, against Italy in the semi-final, but West Germany lost 3-4.

In 1999, Müller was ranked ninth in the European Player of the Century election held by IFFHS.

The best player of the tournament, however, was the one and only Pelé, perhaps the greatest footballer of all time.

In 1958, he had been 17 in Brazil's first World Cup triumph and had been named the Best Young Player. He had watched the 1962 victory mostly from the sidelines after an early injury. The dreams of a Cup hat-trick had come crashing down for the Brazilians during the rough tackles of 1966. The 1970 edition however, was the pinnacle of what is acknowledged to be the greatest football career of all time.

He scored four times, including the 18th minute header that put Brazil ahead in the final against Italy. That brought his tally to 12, and he had scored in all four World Cups.

Born Edson Arantes do Nascimento, Pelé was magical.

Variously known as *A Pérola Negra* (The Black Pearl) or *O Rei do Futebol* (The King of Football), he could beat defenders with speed, fool them with skill, outperform them in air, and had impossible range of vision and creativity. A goalscorer of surreal ability, his anticipation and finishing with both feet were legendary.

And he was beautiful to watch, with his changes of direction, feints and dribbling genius. Later he also became a master playmaker in the midfield.

In all he scored 77 goals for Brazil in 92 matches. In his career, he scored 1281 goals in 1363 games.

During the Mexico World Cup, British television commentator Malcolm Allison asked his colleague: "How do you spell Pele?" Pat Crerand answered: "Easy: G-O-D."

In 1999, the International Federation of Football History & Statistics (IFFHS) voted Pelé the World Player of the Century.

"To play like Pelé is to play like God," said Michel Platini.

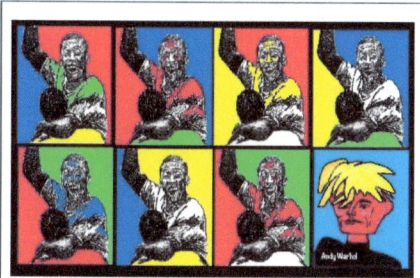

"Pelé is the greatest player in football history, and there will only be one Pelé" Cristiano Ronaldo

"Pelé was one of the few who contradicted my theory: instead of 15 minutes of fame, he will have 15 centuries" Andy Warhol

"The greatest player in history was Di Stefano. I refuse to classify Pelé as a player. He was above that." Ferenc Puskás

"Pele was the only footballer who surpassed the boundaries of logic." Johan Cruijff

"When I saw Pele play, it made me feel I should hang up my boots." Just Fontaine

"I sometimes feel as though football was invented for this magical player" Bobby Charlton

"This debate about the player of the century is absurd. There's only possible answer — Pele. He's the greatest player of all time. And by some distance, I might add." - Zico

"Messi has all the conditions to be the best, but first he has to beat Maradona, Romario and then eventually Pele." - Romario

But what about pointing with the nose and all that?

Altitude, heat, not really advertisement for the organisers.

After life's highs there comes the lows clasp hands behind and point with the nose

Hmm...Let me check...

And atrocious scheduling.

Yes. Just confirmed.

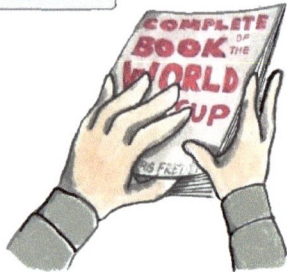

Before the 1970 Cup, when the England team went to Bogota for a warm up game, Bobby Moore was accused of stealing a bracelet. When they returned to Bogota after a match in Ecuador, Moore was held there for four days.

He was innocent.

The accusers and witnesses had different, and obviously falsified, versions of what had happened. The charges were dropped. But Moore had to deal with jibes.

And according to Moore, if he wandered into a jewellery shop, "I had to keep my hands behind my back and point with my nose.

That was after his victory in the 1966 World Cup. Highs and lows.

He's catching on real quick now.

But the blanks don't fit Bobby Moore.

Sonja, could you please type Bogota Bracelet?

Congratulations. You now move to the next question !

Please, please ... you're free to break your heads. But hold on for another 55%

4:00 AM

Groan...

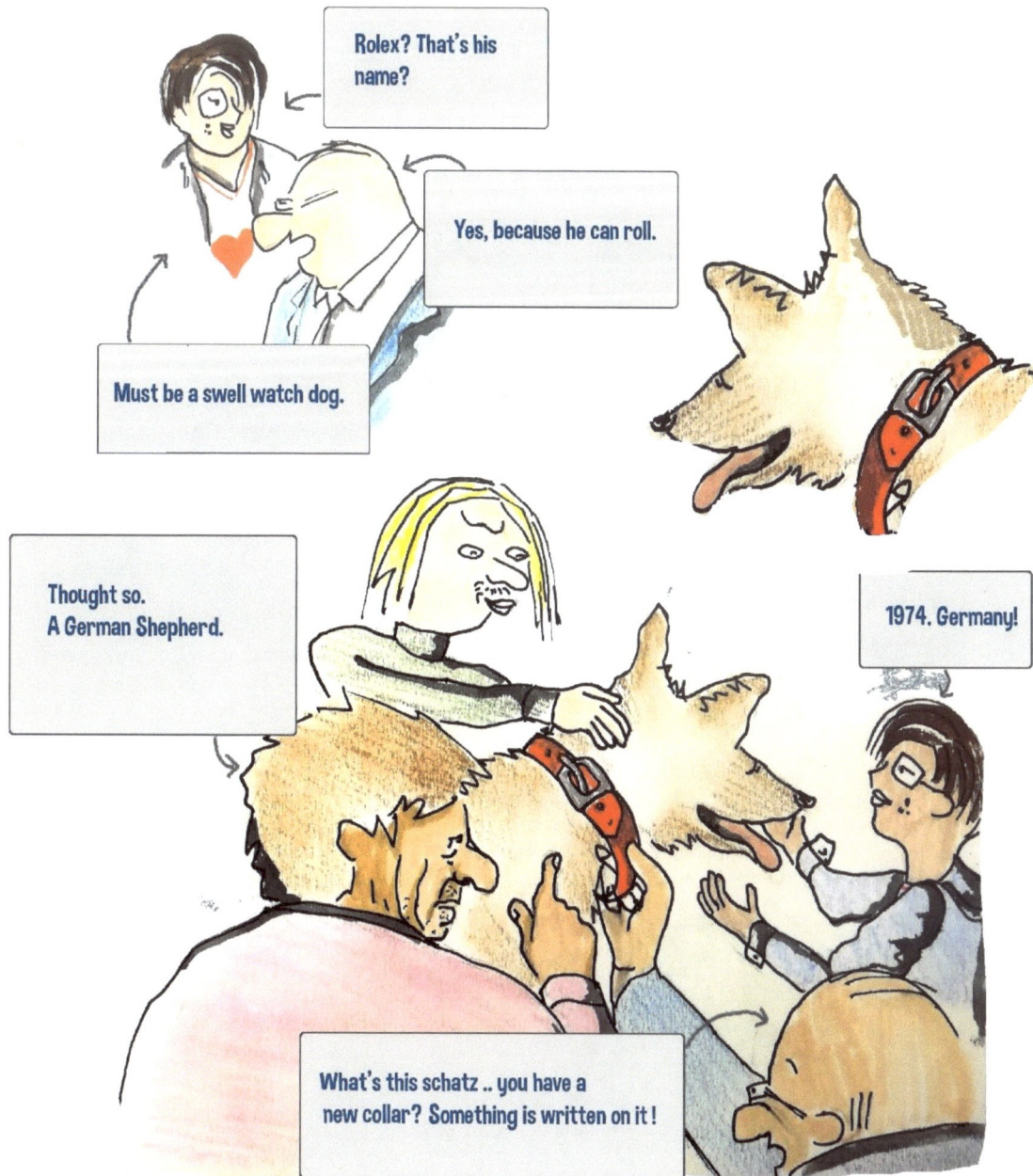

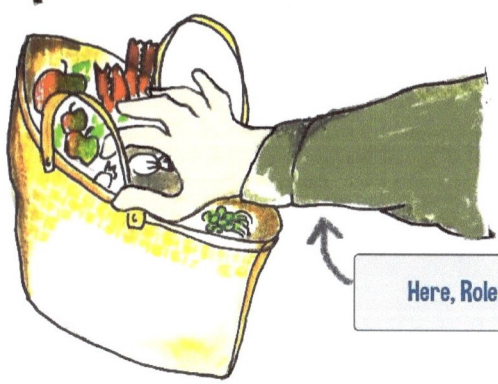

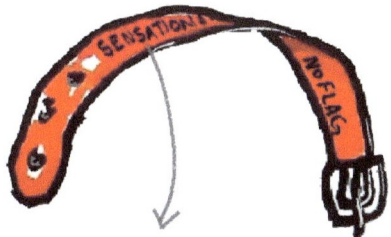

Sensational start after a lag/ 'cause I detected there was no flag

1974, West Germany

Hmmm 1974 ... interesting Cup

Johan Cruijff's Dutchmen were the biggest favourites to win the Cup since the 1954 Hungarians.

And like the men of Puskás, they were stopped at the threshold of the ultimate prize by West Germany, in a historic showdown of two teams showcasing the best of Total Football.

FIFA tinkered around with the format yet again, introducing a second group round after the first. It achieved the rather questionable results of tiring the players and dampening the excitement afforded by another knockout round.

The USSR were disqualified when they refused to appear in the National Stadium in Santiago to play Chile, because the venue had been used as a concentration camp for the political prisoners during Augusto Pinochet's CIA-backed military coup. Chile 'won' the encounter by kicking off and shooting into an empty net.

Because of the recent murders of the Israeli athletes, West Germany beefed up the security forces to the maximum level.

First Round

Group 1

Team	West Germany	Chile	Australia	GF	GA	Pt
East Germany	1-0(0-0)	1-1(0-0)	2-0(0-0)	4	1	5
West Germany		1-0 (1-0)	3-0(2-0)	4	1	4
Chile			0-0(0-0)	1	2	2
Australia				0	5	1

Group 2

Team	Brazil	Scotland	Zaire	GF	GA	Pt
Yugoslavia	0-0(0-0)	1-1(0-0)	9-0(6-0)	10	1	4
Brazil		0-0(0-0)	3-0(1-0)	3	0	4
Scotland			2-0(2-0)	3	1	4
Zaire				0	14	0

Group 3

Team	Sweden	Bulgaria	Uruguay	GF	GA	Pt
Holland	0-0(0-0)	4-1(2-0s)	2-0(1-0)	6	1	5
Sweden		0-0(0-0)	1-0(0-0)	3	0	4
Bulgaria			1-1(0-0)	2	5	2
Uruguay				1	6	1

Group 4

Team	Argentina	Italy	Haiti	GF	GA	Pt
Poland	3-2(2-0)	2-1(2-0)	7-0(5-0)	12	3	6
Argentina		1-1 (1-1)	4-1(2-0)	7	5	3
Italy			3-1(0-0)	5	4	3
Haiti				2	14	0

Highlights:

During the matches involving Chile, the local riot police were busy quelling the demonstrations against the military government back home.

The severe East German defence blocked their neighbours and a long ball in the second half earned them a memorable win. This was the only official encounter between the two Germanys ever.

Defending champion Brazil had to wait for their third match to score their first goals, and those too came against the outsiders, Zaire.

It was after Holland's 4-1 rout of Bulgaria that the world started going crazy about Total Football. The internal differences between the Ajax and Feynoord players in the Dutch side also took a backseat after this game.

Haiti actually managed to take the lead against Italy, and although they lost 1-3 it was a commendable performance. They had promoted the concept of voodoo to help them before the match. However, after this impressive showing Ernst Jean-Joseph became the first player to fail drugs test in a finals tournament.

Second Round

Group A

Team	Brazil	East Germany	Argentina	GF	GA	Pt
Holland	2-0(0-0)	2-0(1-0)	4-0(2-0)	8	0	6
Brazil		1-0 (1-0)	2-1(1-1)	3	3	4
East Germany			1-1(1-1)	1	4	1
Argentina				2	7	1

Group B

Team	Poland	Sweden	Yugoslavia	GF	GA	Pt
West Germany	1-0(0-0)	4-2(0-1)	2-0(1-0)	7	2	6
Poland		1-0(1-0)	2-1(1-1)	3	2	4
Sweden			2-1(1-1)	4	6	2
Yugoslavia				2	6	0

Cruijff's genius came to the fore as Holland crushed Argentina 4-0 and Brazil 2-0 to end the Latin American challenge. Rivelino did score from a fantastic free-kick against East Germany, and Jairzinho and Rivelino recaptured some of the 1970 magic with a brace of goals against Argentina. But Brazil did not go through to the final.

The West Germany-Sweden match was perhaps the best in the tournament. Sweden led by a goal at half-time and a see-saw battle in the second half was finally decided by the German stamina in the last quarter of an hour.

Third Place Final

Poland 1 (0) Brazil 0(0)
Like most third-place matches, this was a dull encounter clinched by the late goal from the eventual top-scorer in the tournament Grzegorz Lato.

Final
West Germany 2 (2) Holland 1 (1)
The Dutch scored in the second minute, from a penalty. And the first German touch on the ball was when they retrieved the ball from the net after Neeskens had drilled it home.
However, Vogts stymied the brilliance of Cruijff with his relentless marking. All the 15 Dutch goals in the tournament either started with a Cruijff move or ended with him putting the ball in the net. Now, with the skipper neutralised, the orange brigade suffered.
Breitner equalised from a penalty, awarded rather controversially to the West Germans, and not for the last time in a final. At the fag end of the first half, the great Gerd Müller who shot in his country's 100th goal in the finals and also the fourteenth and last of his World Cup career.

Holland pressed hard in the second half, but could not get the equaliser in.

Highlights:

Müller retired from football after the final. He became the second man, after the Italian Schiavio in 1934, to bid adieu to the game after scoring the winner in the title round. He finished with 68 goals in 62 matches.

It was a Total Football show in the final, and one of the most hard fought in the history of the Cup.

Top Scorer and Best Player 1974, Germany

He used to race along the right-wing with magnificent acceleration, but years after hanging up his boots went on to become a senator in Poland as a member of the Democratic Left Alliance.

Grzegorz Lato scored twice against Argentina in a shock 3-2 victory in Poland's first match, and then netted two more in the 7-0 rout of Haiti. The team topped the incredibly tough group when they beat Italy 2-1 in the final game. Lato missed that game.

After that Poland played three matches in the second round, and then the third-place final against Brazil. They scored four times in those four matches, Lato netting three of them. Two were with headers, which showed him as effective in the box as he was fast in the wing. The goal that earned Poland the third place was a beauty, with the winger picking the ball inside his own half, breaking into a run and outsprinting the defenders before shooting past the goalkeeper.

Yet, the magical player of the tournament was the Dutch master of innovation, Johan Cruijff.

Marshalling his orange brigade with the fascinating display of Total Football honed during the golden years with Ajax, Cruijff enacted the role of playmaker with his curious change of positions and gift for the perfectly timed pass. He had flawless technique, breath-taking speed, phenomenal acceleration and was a master of dribbling. Yet, what put him ahead of the rest was his tactical vision and creativity.

With Cruijff leading from the front ... and sometimes falling deep behind the front line to confuse the opponents ... Holland cruised through the first round and looked unbeatable in the second. During this phase they routed Argentina 4-0, and made short work of East Germany and defending champions Brazil with a brace of goals against each.

In the final it was essentially due to Cruijff that the first West German to touch the ball was Sepp Maier retrieving it from the net. But after that Bertie Vogts did a splendid job of marking him, and the Franz Beckenbauer led West Germans came back to win it 2-1.

Cruijff later became a coach, with Ajax, Barcelona and then the Catalonia national team. In 1999 he was voted European Player of the Century, and till his death remained as near a cult figure as it is possible to be in The Netherlands.

Let's move on from Cruijff. What about the clue?

It's all about Cruijff.

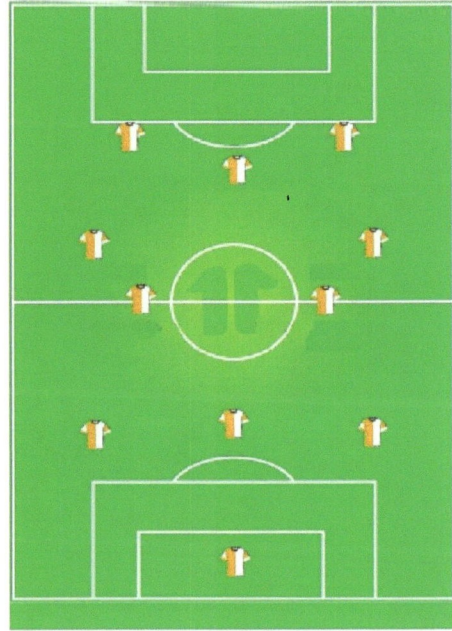

This was the most awaited final, with the Dutch Total Football dominating the world. The final had a most sensational start.

Yes, you said so.

The first German touch was when the goalie retrieved the ball from the net. Was the start delayed?

Yes. By several minutes. Because there was no corner flag.

And who detected it?

The referee. Jack Taylor.

That fits!

Super. You have moved to the next question!

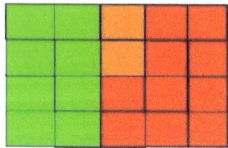

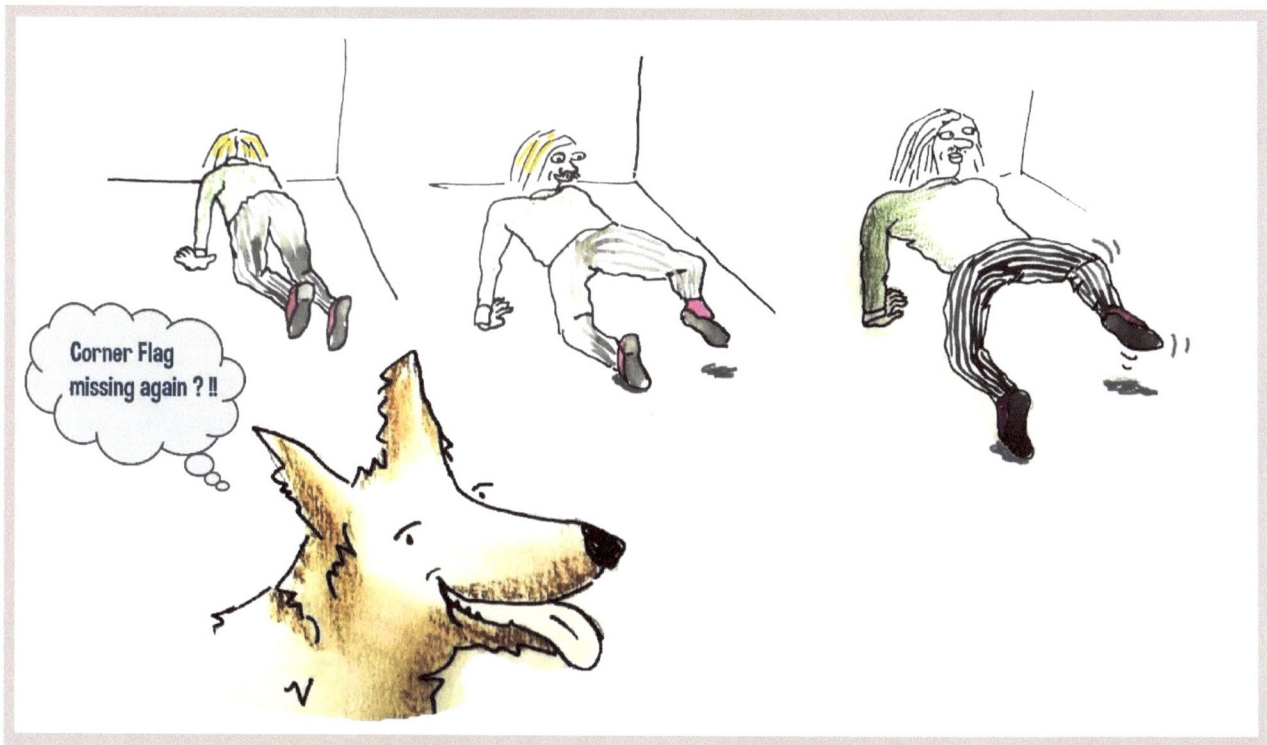

Corner Flag missing again ? !!

5:55 AM

Those two dunderheads are probably sleeping away. They could come over and hand us this one.

CONCEPT

Where did this come from?

Picked it up from the lobby on my way back.

It's yesterday's!

That's strange .. It was lying there as if freshly delivered

Queen Maxima ! ... quick ...

Aber, ... Maxima is the queen of Netherlands

Und .. she comes from Argentina.

Aesthetically ugly, boring and crime/Stupid popularity cannot push my time _ _ _ _ _ _ _ _ _ _ _ _

Here it is !!

Queen Maxima

1978, Argentina

Now let's see what happened in 1978

By the time General Jorge Videla's junta took over the country in a brutal military dictatorship, Argentina had been already identified as the hosts of the 1978 World Cup.

No one had really objected to the Latin American giant hosting the Cup when the decision had been announced. If anything, it had been a belated honour for them. However, with army helicopters buzzing above, submachine guns in the arms of thugs and USA-trained professional torturers going around, teams, especially the Western European ones, were concerned about their safety.

General Actis, the first president of the organising committee, was blown up in an explosion. Even after the Montoneros, one of the main rebel groups, had promised a ceasefire during the tournament, another bomb exploded in a press centre killing a policeman.

However, it was a publicity opportunity for the junta, who spared no expense in hosting the tournament.

The big loss was Johan Cruijff, the Dutch legend, who decided not to travel.

For the second time in a row the hosts won the Cup. However, controversies were aplenty and doubts lingered about the methods used by the Argentinians. The Dutch team, losing finalists for the second consecutive tournament, claimed that it was unlikely that the hosts would have won the Cup unless they had been the 'hosts'.

First Round

Group 1

Team	Argentina	France	Hungary	GF	GA	Pt
Italy	1-0(0-0)	2-1(1-1)	3-1(2-0)	6	2	6
Argentina		2-1 (1-0)	2-1(1-1)	4	3	4
France			3-1(3-1)	5	5	2
Hungary				3	8	0

Group 2

Team	West Germany	Tunisia	Mexico	GF	GA	Pt
Poland	0-0(0-0)	1-0(1-0)	3-1(1-0)	4	1	5
West Germany		0-0(0-0)	6-0(4-0)	6	0	4
Tunisia			3-1(0-1)	3	2	3
Mexico				2	12	0

Group 3

Team	Brazil	Spain	Sweden	GF	GA	Pt
Austria	0-1(0-1)	2-1(1-1)	1-0(1-0)	3	2	4
Brazil		0-0(0-0)	1-1(1-1)	2	1	4
Spain			1-0(0-0)	2	2	3
Sweden				1	3	1

Group 4

Team	Holland	Scotland	Iran	GF	GA	Pt
Peru	0-0(0-0)	3-1(1-1)	4-1(3-1)	7	2	5
Holland		2-3 (1-1)	3-0(1-0)	5	3	3
Scotland			1-1(1-0)	5	6	3
Iran				2	8	1

Highlights:

Argentina won their first two matches against Hungary and France by slim 2-1 margins, and were helped in both the cases by poor refereeing.

Because of black and white TV, one of the teams had to play in light stripes and the other in dark. This led to the Hungary-France match being delayed till the local football club Kimberley came to the rescue lending French players their green and white jerseys.

After referee Avraham Klein of Israel prevented any further advantage to the home team in their match against Italy, which Argentina lost 0-1, the hosts prevented him from being the official in any of their remaining matches.

With Brazil and Sweden tied 1-1, six seconds into stoppage time and the ball in the air, referee Clive Thomas blew the final whistle and walked out, oblivious to the fact that Zico's header was sailing into the net. The match went down as a draw.

Tunisia became the first African country to win a finals match when they came back from behind to beat Mexico 3-1.

A huge proportion of the pitches on which the matches were played were atrocious.

Second Round

Group A

Team	Italy	West Germany	Austria	GF	GA	Pt
Holland	2-1(0-1)	2-2(1-1)	5-1(3-0)	9	4	5
Italy		0-0 (0-0)	1-0(1-0)	2	2	3
West Germany			2-3(1-0)	4	5	2
Austria				4	8	2

Group B

Team	Brazil	Poland	Peru	GF	GA	Pt
Argentina	0-0(0-0)	2-0(1-0)	6-0(2-0)	8	0	5
Brazil		3-1(1-1)	3-0(2-0)	6	1	5
Poland			1-0(0-0)	2	5	2
Peru				0	10	0

The Dutch display against Austria was one of the flawless demonstrations of Total Football.

The West Germany versus Holland match was one of the best in the tournament, with the Germans taking the lead twice with the Dutch equalising the second time with seven minutes left in the game.

With Brazil and Argentina playing out a goalless draw, the teams were level on points when they began their respective final matches. Brazil was slightly ahead on the goal difference. However, Argentina's match against Peru started later than the Brazil-Poland encounter, and hence the hosts knew that they had to win by a minimum three-goal margin while scoring at least four. Ultimately they trounced Peru 6-0. Was it true that the Peruvian goalkeeper Ramón Quiroga, a naturalised Argentinian, had helped out his native land? The Brazilians thought so. Besides, there were rumours of £50 million being funded into the Peruvian economy as Argentinian aid. But, Quiroga did make some excellent saves, and Peru hit the post almost as soon as the match started.

It was more of the brilliance of Mário Kempes who had entered a purple patch that saw the hosts through. Not insignificant was the diving header of Tarantini, which gave him his only goal in international matches.

Third Place Final

Brazil 2 (0) Italy 1(1)

Refereed by Klein because the Argentinians did not want him in the final, this match saw an erstwhile rough Brazil team play their best football. Trailing at the break, they shot ahead through two long rangers, the equaliser by Nelinho one of the most incredible swerving strikes ever seen.

Final

Argentina 3 (1,1) Holland 1 (0,1)

The Dutch were not as good as the 1974 side, but they emulated Cruijff's great team by reaching the final. There was quite a lot of poor refereeing in the title round, with blind eyes greeting many of the handballs effected by the hosts in the second half. A late equaliser put them at par, and in the injury time Rensenbrink's prod hit the post.

In the extra time Kempes outran two men in a spectacular run and then scored off a lucky rebound. Five minutes from the final whistle, Bertoni made it 3-1 off another lucky bounce.

Highlights:

Holland became the first country to lose consecutive finals.

Daniel Passarella, the Argentinian captain, received the trophy from the infamous George Jorge Rafael Videla.

Top Scorer and Best Player 1978, Argentina

He took his time to get going. It was the second World Cup for the attacking central midfielder, and he was well into his 11th match during Argentina's second round game against Poland.

It was then that Mario Kempes scored his first goal in the finals. A perfectly timed diagonal run to meet a left-wing cross with a near post header. However, after that no one could stop him. He netted his second goal in the same match.

In the same game, he also stopped a goal with his hand. The resulting penalty was saved by Ubaldo Fillol.

After playing the 1974 World Cup as a teenager, Kempes had matured into a dangerous goal scorer in Spain, becoming a star for Valencia. The brace against Poland broke a dam of sorts. After that Kempes kept finding the goal again and again.

Against Peru, in the final group match, he scored two more in a 6-0 triumph.

Then came the final against the Dutchmen. Kempes burst between the defenders and stabbed the ball under the goalkeeper to open put Argentina ahead. The regulation time ended with the teams locked 1-1. And in the 104th minute he scored again, once again storming through the defence and plugged it home after Jan Jongbloed had blocked his first strike.

He was the architect of the third goal as well, when another barrelling run from the deep led to another ricochet which was slammed in by Daniel Bartoni.

Argentina won 3-1 and Kempes, with six goals, became both the highest scorer and the best player of the tournament. Along with Garrincha in 1962 and Rossi in 1982, he remains in the select club of footballers to win both the Golden Boot and Golden Ball awards.

Nicknamed *El Toro* and *EL Matador*, Kempes was noted for his skill, speed and courage, and also had extraordinary composure.

Indeed. In *Esse Est Percipi* he says that soccer in Argentina has ceased to be a sport and entered the realm of spectacle. By Jove! He held a lecture in Buenos Aires which clashed with Argentina's opening game against Hungary He refused to change his schedule.

Stupid popularity cannot push my time

Type it fast. One minute remains

Jorge Luis Borges

Just in time. You have moved to the next question !

PHEW !

- 46 -

The fall to make them outsider, act of disgrace?/Not a happy death, but instigated by race?

— — — — — — —

1982, Spain

Hmmm... let me look back at 1982

There were 24 teams, a brainchild, if it can be called so, of João Havelange. The attempt to have a mix of league and knockout was even more ridiculous now.

Three of the sides were from the British Isles.

The Brazil side looked as close to the Giants of 1970s as possible, and along with the 1954 Hungarians and the 1974 Dutch, they became the third absolute favourites not to win the Cup. They were knocked out in a classic virtual quarter-final encounter against Italy, one of the greatest football games of all time.

Italy, on their part, looked pedestrian and hardly likely to win a match, let alone the Cup, before Paolo Rossi, the forward caught up in all sorts of controversies, transformed them into a champion outfit.

First Round

Group 1

Team	Italy	Cameroon	Peru	GF	GA	Pt
Poland	0-0(0-0)	0-0(0-0)	5-1(0-0)	5	1	4
Italy		1-1 (0-0)	1-1(1-0)	2	2	3
Cameroon			0-0(0-0)	1	1	3
Peru				2	6	2

Group 2

Team	Austria	Algeria	Chile	GF	GA	Pt
West Germany	1-0(1-0)	1-2(0-0)	4-1(1-0)	6	3	4
Austria		2-0(0-0)	1-0(1-0)	3	1	4
Algeria			3-2(3-0)	5	5	4
Chile				3	8	0

Group 3

Team	Argentina	Hungary	El Salvador	GF	GA	Pt
Belgium	1-0(0-0)	1-1(0-1)	1-0(1-0)	3	1	5
Argentina		4-1(2-0)	2-0(1-0)	6	2	4
Hungary			10-1(3-0)	12	6	3
El Salvador				1	13	0

Group 4

Team	France	Czechoslovakia	Kuwait	GF	GA	Pt
England	3-1(1-1)	2-0(0-0)	1-0(1-0)	6	1	6
France		1-1(0-0)	4-1(2-0)	6	5	3
Czechoslovakia			1-1(1-0)	2	4	2
Kuwait				2	6	1

Group 5

Team	Spain	Yugoslavia	Honduras	GF	GA	Pt
Northern Ireland	1-0(0-0)	0-0(0-0)	1-1(0-1)	2	1	4
Spain		2-1(1-1)	1-1(0-1)	3	3	3
Yugoslavia			1-0(0-0)	2	2	3
Honduras				2	3	2

Group 6

Team	France	Czechoslovakia	Kuwait	GF	GA	Pt
England	3-1(1-1)	2-0(0-0)	1-0(1-0)	6	1	6
France		1-1(0-0)	4-1(2-0)	6	5	3
Czechoslovakia			1-1(1-0)	2	4	2
Kuwait				2	6	1

Highlights:

The Cameroon-Italy match was the last ever played in the finals without substitutes from either side.

There were just 10 goals in the six games of Group 1, six of which came in the second half of the Poland-Peru encounter. Italy, the eventual champions, squeezed through past Cameroon after being level on points and goal difference by having scored two goals to the latter's one. Very seldom has any World Cup winning side made a more sedate start.

The Algerians shocked West Germany and then lost steam against Austria. However, when the West Germany-Austria match was played in an extremely desultory manner producing an outcome which pitchforked the two neighbouring countries into the next round while ending the journey for the African nation, the Algerians had every right to feel aggrieved.

Diego Maradona was severely guarded through the games of Argentina, but nevertheless managed to score twice against Hungary.

Hungary's 10-1 win against El Salvador set the record for the highest number of goals by one team in a World Cup match.

During their match against France, the powerful Kuwaiti Sheikh Fahad Al-Sabah, in his colourful robes, called his players off the pitch to protest against a goal awarded to the opponents. Referee Miroslav Stupar actually disallowed the goal under pressure. He was not allowed to referee any match after that.

Second Round

Group A

Team	USSR	Belgium	GF	GA	Pt
Poland	0-0(0-0)	3-0(2-0)	3	0	3
USSR		1-0 (0-0)	1	0	3
Belgium			0	4	0

Group B

Team	England	Spain	GF	GA	Pt
West Germany	0-0(0-0)	2-1 (0-0)	2	1	3
England		0-0 (0-0)	0	0	2
Spain			1	2	1

Group C

Team	Brazil	Argentina	GF	GA	Pt
Italy	3-2(2-1)	3-1(1-0)	5	3	4
Brazil		2-1 (0-0)	5	4	2
Argentina			2	5	0

Group D

Team	Austria	Northern Ireland	GF	GA	Pt
France	1-0(1-0)	4-1(1-0)	5	1	4
Austria		2-2 (0-1)	2	3	1
Northern Ireland			3	6	1

Highlights

Paolo Rossi's hat-trick stopped the great Brazil side of Zico, Socrates and Falcao in their tracks. The Brazilians, the greatest assembled since 1970, drew level twice, but Rossi struck once too often. That was the game that made the world, including the Italians and their team, suddenly realise that they were serious contenders.

Maradona's World Cup came to an end three minutes earlier than schedule when he was sent off against Brazil for some fouls resulting from frustrations. In the match against Italy, Claudio Gentile had kept him quiet through repeated shoving, pushing and tugging at the shirt.

At the other end of the spectrum, England went out of the World Cup after two drab, dry goalless draws against West Germany and Spain.

Semi-finals

Italy 2 (1) Poland 0 (0)

Rossi, mojo unlocked, kept scoring. He did so twice in this match. There seemed little the rest of the remaining contenders could do to stop him.

West Germany 3 (1,1) France 3 (1,1) Tie-breaker West Germany 5 France 4

The most dramatic match in the Cup. The Germans had taken an early lead and a Michel Platini penalty had put France on level footing. The teams were locked 1-1 at half time and full time. France scored twice during the first nine minutes of extra-time, and seemed to be cruising towards the final. However, Karl-Heinz Rummenigge, coming in at the 97th minute, made it 3-2 and then Fischer pummelled an overhead kick to draw level once again.

West Germany went through in the tie-breaker, the excellent match marred only by Schumacher's violent body-check on Battiston. The results were concussion and broken teeth on one side and complete lack of punishment in the form of either booking or free-kick on the other.

Third-Place Final

Poland 3 (2) France 2 (1)

One of the rare entertaining third place finals. The result could have been different if France had not decided to give most of their reserves a game.

Final

Italy 3 (0) West Germany 1 (0)

Even a missed penalty did not stop Italy from overcoming the Germans with plenty to spare. It did help that captain Rummenigge was not fully fit and still limped through 70 minutes of the match.

After a goalless first half, there was a sense of inevitability as Rossi netted the first goal. By the time Breitner managed to perform the near-impossible of beating the 40-year-old Dino Zoff, it was already too late.

Highlights:

The match against Italy saw West Germany losing against a European country for the first time since the 1978 finals.

Rummenigge's insistence to play in spite of injury was severely criticised by the teammate Uli Stielike.

Chaos marred much of the organisation of the tournament, culminating in the Spanish police force clubbing the photographers trying to take pictures of the final presentation.

Top Scorer and Best Player 1982, Spain

In the 1978 World Cup, three goals and four assists had won this slightly built centre-forward a place in the team of the tournament and the honour of being judged the second best player of the tournament. Soon after that Lanerossi Vicenza offered 2.612 billion lire to buy him off Juventus, making Paolo Rossi the most expensive player of the world.

But within another season, he was caught up in the infamous Totonero, and was thus banned for three years. Juventus bought him back in spite of the ban.

Leading up to the 1982 World Cup, Italian scribes and fans judged Rossi to be in very poor shape. And as Italy just about got through to the second round after listless draws against Poland, Cameroon and Peru, he was described as 'a ghost aimlessly wandering over the field'.

But Enzo Bearzot was adamant that the quick, agile and elegant forward was a key component of his plans. With Argentina and Brazil in their group in the second round, the task was cut out. Rossi did little in the 2-1 win over Argentina. And then Italy faced the star-studded Brazil with a line-up including men like Sócrates, Zico, and Falcão.

Rossi headed in the first goal. Sócrates equalised. Rossi made it 2-1 with a steal from the edge of the penalty area. It was another 43 minutes before Falcão screamed in delight on making it 2-2.

But six minutes later Rossi swivelled to anticipate a pass from a corner and shot from the six-yard line to make it 3-2. That was the final scoreline of one of the greatest games of the World Cup.

In the semi-final it was Poland again, and this time Rossi netted two more in the one-sided victory.

In the final, it remained goalless till the 56th minute before Rossi's header into an empty net put Italy in the lead. He had now scored the last six goals for Italy. Eventually they won 3-1. Rossi became the third player, after Garrincha and Kempes and the last so far, to be both the Top Scorer and Best Player. With the Golden Shoe and the Golden Ball awards established from this edition, he carried both away.

Fall to make them outsider, act of disgrace... Was it Schumacher bodychecking Battison in the semi finals?

Did he die?

No. It wouldn't have been a happy death anyway.

And a German becoming violent against French. History is littered with this, but it is hardly anything to do with race.

10 minutes left, guys. Hurry.

Fall, Outsider, Happy Death ... the guy keeps coming back to literature.

Here's another outsider begging for an unhappy death...

We are talking Camus here.

Albert Camus? You know that he used to be a goalkeeper. For Racing Universitaire d'Alger... till he contracted tuberculosis at the age of 17.

Good heavens. Camus.

Algeria !!

THE MYTH

the Stranger Albert Camus

THE FALL ALBERT CAMUS

ALBERT CAMUS

A Happy Death

ALGERIA

When Austria and West Germany played the last group match, a draw or a win for Austria or a 3-0 win for West Germany would have put Algeria through to the next round. But the Germans scored early and the rest of the match was played with lacklustre aimlessness It was called the Disgrace of Gijón, or Anschluss - a reference to the 1938 Austria-Germany pact The neighbouring countries went through, while Algeria was left in the cold Many, including commentators and players, hinted at match-fixing Algerian fans even waved dollar bills from the stands implying the same. Some said it was European nations teaming up against an African one... hence instigated by race.

Correct ! Now you have 60% of your funds transferred back to your account.

> Has agents who bring clues inside FIFA building.
> Has planned it over a considerable period
> Knows phone numbers of Fassler, Hernandez…
> Literature lover

Psychiatric profiling says:

"A single individual, not a gang"

He is a reader … probably a collector of books. Javier, I think you should look for deliveries of loads of books to one particular location.

That results in too huge a suspect list

Not necessarily …

… our man will be…

buying books

on football

Literature around the world

modern classics

cryptography

codes

hacking

Kindle e-readers

Truck loads of Amazon deliveries

abe books…

second hand book stores

Poetry

If we join all these parameters … the probable suspects will diminish rapidly..

Brilliant... !

I don't have concrete evidence, but there is a good chance of him being an Englishman who has spent much of his time in United States.

Indeed? Why so?

Who else will be this passionate about football, use Bernard Shaw and the Queen in his clues, communicate literary gems from different languages and write couplets in English and yet ... yet think of pickled cucumber as 'Pickles'.

♪ mmhmm·· English man ·· in·· ·· mm hm·· New York··

··Be yourself no matter what they say...

... yes, some new angles to capture

But it is ten. The next clue?... and speaking as a real Englishman who lives in England, I could do with some tea ...

Whoa ... who brought this in?

A cleaning lady.. !

Her name tag said Sofia Garcia. I am sure she was Mexican.

Ticket prices, Celsius, Altitude alike/There's always TV, spectators can take a hike.

— — — — — —

Can the team crack this cryptic puzzle? Can they recover the rest of the money?
Or will the World Cup be in jeopardy?

Who is this curious adversary they are up against? Will he play fair?
To find out more you must read the next volumes of SUDDEN DEATH

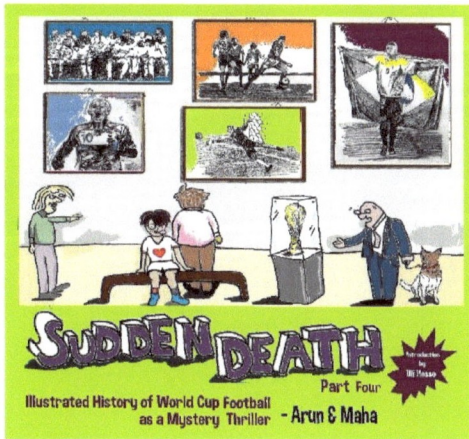

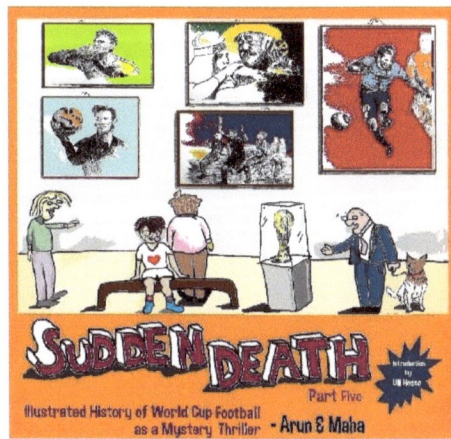

A Product of the Blinders Team

www.ingramcontent.com/pod-product-compliance
Lightning Source LLC
LaVergne TN
LVHW072117070426
835510LV00003B/100